Miss FRANCES'
ALL-DAY-LONG
BOOK

by Dr. Frances R. Horwich

and Reinald Werrenrath, Jr.

Illustrations by Katherine Evans

RAND McNALLY & COMPANY

New York • CHICAGO • San Francisco

TO PARENTS

The *All-Day-Long Book* was written to give children and their parents ideas of activities appropriate for different times of the day. We all know that certain kinds of play are better suited to one time of day than to another. For example, a child should be encouraged to enjoy quiet, relaxing activities in the periods before bedtime, naptime, or mealtime. Since it may be necessary to interrupt these play periods, it is best to plan with your child on short activities for these times.

Throughout the book we have used the technique of asking direct questions, as a means of helping children to think about certain things as you read this material to them.

For the children, much of the information will come from the pictures. However, by reading the text to them you will stimulate "thinking together" and "doing together," both of which are extremely valuable to the child's social development and to your relationship with your child.

We hope that you and your children have many happy days together, enjoying these activities of Ding Dong School.

Frances R. Horwich
Reinald Werrenrath, Jr.

CAN YOU name some of the things you do in the morning? In the afternoon? In the evening? What are some of the things you do all day long?

There are times, before your nap or before lunch or dinner, when it is fun to do quiet things, and other times when it is fun to work or play hard. Are there some times when you like to play alone and other times when you like to play with a friend?

In Ding Dong School we do many interesting things together. They are things that you may do afterward, at different times of the day.

Whatever you do or whenever you play, have fun!

Miss Frances

THINGS TO DO IN THE MORNING

ALONE OR WITH A FRIEND

WHEN Mother is talking on the telephone, feeding the baby, or busy in the kitchen, there are many things that you can do by yourself or with a friend.

Sometimes you will want to do these things in the morning. Other days you may want to do them in the afternoon or before supper. There is no one "best" time for them. However, all of these are fun to do alone or with a friend:

Talk on your toy telephone

Play with your train

Look at books

Make a picture

Play with your dolls

Build with your blocks

The pictures will tell you what they are.

Your Toy Telephone

DO YOU feel like calling someone on your toy telephone? Who shall it be?

Pretend you are calling the man in the market. Tell him all the different things you need—eggs, lettuce, strawberries, bread, milk, and soap flakes.

Or you may want to pretend that you are talking to your friend the policeman or the fireman.

Do you have a very good friend that you can call on your toy telephone, to find out if he would like to come over and play? Did he ask his mother if he could come?

Play with Your Train

SOME toy trains have tracks. Others slide along on the floor. You can have fun playing with either kind. Which do you have?

Do you want your train to be a streamliner and go fast? Or is it a slow train?

Where are the passengers?

How does the train whistle sound?

Are there gates at the crossing?

When you want your train to go the other way, how do you turn it around?

When it is time to stop playing with your train, where do you put it? Find a good place, so that someone won't step on it.

Where did you put it? I can't see it.

Look at Books

WHERE do you keep your books? Can you reach them? Now is a good time to sit down and look at your books. First go and get two of them. You choose the two that you want.

Take your books and sit down in a warm and comfortable place. Will it be your own chair? Do you like to sit on the floor and look at books? Or do you want to sit in a big chair?

Wherever you sit, be sure you have enough space so that you can turn the pages.

Maybe you will have time to look at another book. Which one will it be?

Make a Picture

WOULD you like to make a picture? How about making one to give to your Daddy when he comes home from work? Should it be a little picture or a big picture? Maybe you would like to draw it on newspaper.

You need your crayons. Where are they?

Now, with your crayons and paper, you are ready. Maybe you want to make a picture of your house, your bed, your friend, or your train.

When your picture is finished, put it away carefully. Then when Daddy comes home you may give it to him. He will be happy when he sees it.

Play with Your Dolls

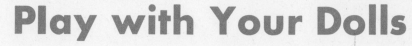

WHEN you are with a friend, why don't you play with your dolls? Each of you take one doll. There are many things you can do for them.

How about a doll party with your dishes?

Or taking the dolls for a walk around your room?

Or giving the dolls a pretend bath?

Or telling a story to your dolls?

Or making a picture for your dolls?

Each one of these is fun for you and your friend. I am sure you and your friend can think of more things to do with your dolls.

What is the name of your doll? Have you introduced your friend to your dolls?

Build with Your Blocks

DO YOU have different kinds of blocks? Some big ones and some small ones? Are they wood, or cardboard, or plastic?

For some buildings you will need all your different kinds of blocks. What would you like to build? A railroad station? A new apartment building? A fence and barn?

A railroad station is a big, long building. At some railroad stations the trains go inside the train shed and at others they stop outside the station. Which kind will yours be? How long will it be? Will it have a tower on one end?

What else does a railroad station have? A platform, where people get on the train. A big door and some windows.

An express wagon to carry the baggage.

Is your station ready? Because here comes the train!

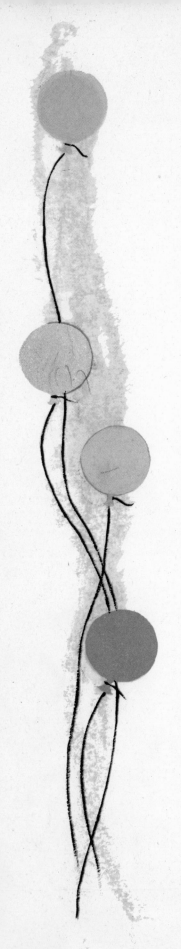

THINGS TO DO

WITH MOTHER OR DADDY

WHEN the weather is nice there are many things you can do outdoors if Mother or Daddy is with you. Here are a few:

Take a walk down the street

Make ice cream

Build a house of boxes

Go for a trip

Make a snowman

You can think of many more, can't you?

When you play indoors with Mother or Daddy, here are other things you can do:

Bathe your doll

Spot paint

Shoe-box train

Make butter

Sew with jingle bells

Handkerchief tricks

You can't do all of these things on the same day. It is a good idea to plan what you are going to do with Mother and Daddy.

Walk down the Street

DO YOU like to play outdoors when your mother or daddy is working in the yard?

If you go for a walk or a ride on your tricycle, be sure to tell your mother about it before you go. Then she will know where you are. That is very important, isn't it?

I know you will remember not to cross an alley or a street, won't you? You cross streets when someone older is with you.

What do you see when you go down the street? Are there some cars, and a fire hydrant? Are there houses, or apartment buildings? Did you ever count the houses? You can tell someone at home about the things you see when you go down the street.

What do you do when you come to the curb at the end of the block? You turn around and come right back home again, don't you?

Maybe later, when you come back home, you will have time to draw a picture of one thing you saw. Would you like to do that?

Make Ice Cream

SOMEDAY, instead of buying ice cream at the store, it would be fun to make it at home. However, there are certain things you must have in order to make it.

You need an ice-cream freezer.
You need a lot of finely chopped ice.
You need some rock salt.
You need the things to cook together
   which make the ice cream.

Here is the recipe for ice cream:

Mix together: 1 quart cream (scalded)
             $\frac{3}{4}$ cup sugar
Cool, and then add: $1\frac{1}{2}$ teaspoons vanilla
             $\frac{1}{8}$ teaspoon salt
Freeze in an ice-cream freezer, using five
   parts of ice to one part of rock salt.

It takes quite a long time (fifteen or twenty minutes) for it to thicken. You will have fun singing and making up rhymes while you take turns at cranking the freezer.

You know who will scrape the dasher when the ice cream is frozen!

Build a House of Boxes

DO YOU remember where there are any big cardboard boxes you can use to build a house?

If you can find several boxes you can make a big house. If you only have one large box you may want to open the end and make a house big enough to crawl inside.

Are you inside? Do you hear someone knocking on the door?

Perhaps you can find an old hatbox to use. It would make a nice round top for your house. Or it can be a small house and you can play around the outside of it.

Go for a Trip

DO YOU want to take a trip somewhere? What about a trip to the beach? Perhaps you would like to go to the park.

Who will go with you—your mother, your brother or sister? You would like someone to play with you, wouldn't you?

What will you need to wear? Your bathing suit or a play suit. You will want a hat and some old shoes or sandals. What else do you want to take? A beach ball or a large ball of any kind will be fun to play with. If you take a balloon with a long string you can fly it in the wind. You must hold on to the string or the balloon will fly away.

When you are there, you can do many things with your beach ball. Someone may toss it to you. Can you catch it when it bounces? It's fun to roll the ball to someone, too.

There is a lot of sand at the beach, and sometimes there is a sandbox at the park. Do you like to dig and build things in the sand?

If you build a long ramp of sand, the ball will roll down by itself. You can make a curved ramp or a straight ramp. Make a hole at the bottom of the ramp and see if you can make the ball roll into it. When your ball rolls into the hole you can bury the ball, and then see if you can find it again.

Did you find it?

Make a Snowman

WHEN it snows and is cold outside, that is the time to make a snowman. You will need a lot of snow, and it must be just right, so that when you roll it in a ball it will stick. Before you go outdoors look at yourself. Are you wearing boots, snowsuit, cap, and mittens? Make sure you are dressed so you won't get cold or wet.

First, make a snowball, and then roll it in the snow until it gets bigger and bigger. You need a great big snowball for the bottom of the snowman.

When that ball is finished, roll another one.
Maybe someone can help you. This snowball
doesn't need to be quite so big as the first.
Then both of you will put this snowball on top
of the first one.

Now what do you need? Of course, one
more, smaller, snowball for the snowman's
head. That won't take so long to roll.

There is the snowman, ready for you to
add his eyes, nose, and mouth. Are there any
small branches or stones that you can use?

Stand back and look at the snowman. Is
he bigger than you?

Bathe Your Doll

MAYBE someday you will want to give one of your dolls a bath. Check with Mother to be sure that your doll can be put in water.

You and Mother together can find the best place to bathe your doll. There are several things you will need. A tub of water, soap, washcloth, and towel for the doll. For yourself you will need an apron or smock.

Be sure you get your doll clean. Don't forget her neck, ears, hands, and legs, and try not to let the soap get in her eyes. You know how that feels, don't you?

After her bath—will you dress your doll for a walk or for her nap?

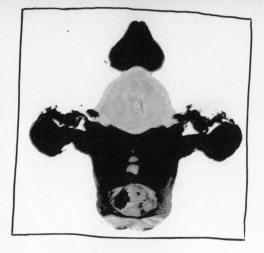
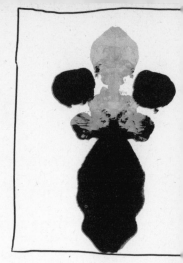

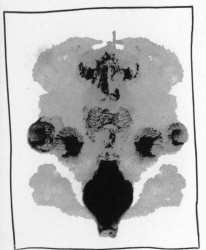

Spot Paint

ON THIS page are some spot paintings.

What do they look like? A bird? A butterfly? Or just a design?

A spot painting is a picture you can make with paper and thick, water-base paint. The best place to do this kind of painting is on the kitchen table or on oilcloth. You need a spoon or stick to dip the paint out of the jar.

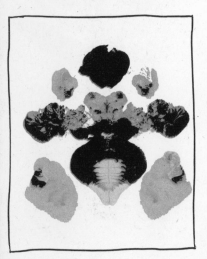

Dip some paint out of the jar and put it right in the middle of the paper. Very carefully fold the paper, and press down gently to make it stay. Can you feel the lump of paint with your finger? Press on the lump and spread it out slowly with your finger. You are making your design now, but you can't really see it, can you? Guess what it will look like when you unfold the paper. Now pick up one corner, very gently, and open it. Are you surprised?

Shoe-Box Train

DO YOU want to make a train of your own to play with? All you need are a few empty shoe boxes for cars, and some string to tie them together. You will need your blunt scissors to cut the string, too.

How many shoe boxes do you want on your train? Three or four? Either one is a good number. Now make a hole in each end of each box. With a short piece of string you can tie each box to the next one. Tie them close together. You may need some help with this.

Which end of the train is the front? Does your train have an engine? Tie a long piece of string to the front box so you can pull your cars. You are the engineer.

Now load the train, Mr. Engineer. What will you put in the cars, wooden blocks? Your stuffed animals? Your dolls? Your small automobiles? All set? Pull the train to the first stop. It is time to unload.

Where are you going next, Mr. Engineer?

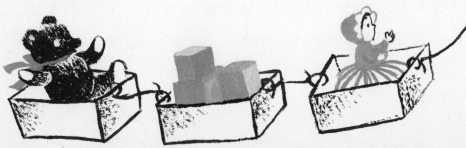

Make Butter

SOMETIMES we buy butter in a store and sometimes we make it at home. If you have never made butter, you might try. It is lots of fun.

You can make butter from whipping cream you buy in the store or get from the milkman. You need a mixing bowl and an egg beater.

Pour the cream into the bowl, and someone can help you start beating it with the egg beater. If you make it go too fast it may spatter the cream out of the bowl.

You can say this little rhyme as you beat:

Come, butter, come,
Come, butter, come!
Margaret's at the garden gate,
Waiting with her butter plate.
Come, butter, come.

Take turns with the beating, because it takes time to turn the cream into butter. First the cream will become thick. Keep right on beating. Then you will see some yellow butter in the cream—just a little at first—then more and more. There will be some liquid, too. Pour this into a glass or cup.

Do you have some toast to spread the butter on? Does it taste good?

Sew with Jingle Bells

YOU KNOW what jingle bells are, don't you?

Ask someone to thread a big needle with a piece of yarn or string. The string should be as long as your arms when you stretch them out. Then you can help sew some jingle bells on the string. When there are enough bells on the string, put it around your neck. If you dance around, the bells will jingle.

Now take the same string of bells and wind it around a stick. The stick should be about twelve inches long. Someone can tie the string so that it will stay. You can shake this just as you would a rattle. Try shaking it with the music of one of your records.

In the kitchen is there a mixing spoon with slits in it? Perhaps you may borrow it for a while. Someone can help you sew bells in and around the slits. When they are fastened, you take the handle of the spoon and shake it. What does it sound like? You and your friends will have lots of fun playing with jingle bells.

Handkerchief Tricks

DO YOU have a large handkerchief? There are several things you can make with it.

How many corners does your handkerchief have? Count them—one, two, three, four. It is a square, isn't it? Now fold the handkerchief so that it has only three corners. Count them to be sure—one, two, three. Now it is a triangle! What can you do with it?

Here is a way to make a rabbit with long ears. Perhaps someone can make one first. Then it will be your turn.

Put your handkerchief on a table and fold it so that it has three corners. Now put your hand on the table, with the palm down, and slide it under the long straight side that you folded. Lift your hand up, but don't turn it over. The handkerchief doesn't look like a rabbit yet, does it? Rabbits have long ears on the top of their heads. How can you make the points of the handkerchief look like the rabbit's ears?

Pull the two end points up under your hand, tuck one between your thumb and forefinger and the other between your fourth and little finger, and pull the points through.

Now your rabbit has ears! If you wiggle your fingers a little, it will make your rabbit's nose wiggle.

Try to make a smaller triangle from the big triangle by folding the handkerchief again. How many points does it have? Fold it into a smaller triangle, and a smaller one, and a smaller one.

There are lots of other things you can do with a handkerchief. Maybe someone can show you how to tie a knot with it. Or perhaps someone will make a cap for you by tying a small knot in each corner.

Where did your rabbit go?

THINGS TO DO

BEFORE YOUR NAP

AFTER lunch is the time to get ready for your nap. You want quiet and restful things to do. You have just a few minutes to play, so you want things that don't take very long. Let's think of some.

> Listen to one or two records
>
> Look at a book
>
> Water your plants
>
> Play with your puzzle
>
> Put your doll to bed
>
> Sing a song

After you have done only one of these, it will be time for you to get ready for your nap. So off you go quietly and get ready. When you are in bed, close your eyes and sleep. After you wake up you will have many other things to do.

Listen to Some Records

YOU DON'T have very much time, because soon you will take your nap. Choose one or two of your records. Then sit on the floor or a hassock or in a chair and listen. Maybe you would like to sing along with the record.

The time before your nap is a quiet time, and sitting and listening to records is quiet and restful, isn't it?

Which two records do you want to play? Is this one your favorite record?

Look at a Book

IF YOU don't want to listen to records, why not look at a book? You find the one you want and then the best place to sit quietly and look at the pictures. Maybe you want to tell the story as you turn the pages.

When you are finished, what time will it be? Of course—naptime. So be sure to put the book away.

Have a good nap, and there will be more things to do when you wake up.

Water Your Plants

IF YOU haven't watered your plants yet today, maybe this is a good time to do it.

What kind of plants do you have? A pumpkin vine? A sweet-potato plant?

What do you use to water your plants? You can use a small pitcher or a small watering can. Either one works very well. Remember to be careful so that all the water goes into the flower pot. If a little water spills, you must wipe it up with a cloth, a sponge, or a paper towel.

Sometimes if your plant is up high and you can't reach it you will need some help. Be sure you ask someone to help you.

You didn't spill any water, did you?

Play with Your Puzzle

YOU KNOW what a puzzle is, don't you? It has several pieces that fit together to make a picture or a design. Do you have a puzzle of your own? Go and find your favorite puzzle now and we will play with it.

First, take all the pieces out of your puzzle. How many do you have? Can you count them? Spread them out so that you can see each shape. Each one is a different shape, isn't it? Is it a different color, too?

Now put all the pieces back together. Do they all fit? Does your puzzle look just the same as it did before? Is this one still your favorite puzzle?

Where do you keep your puzzle? On a shelf or in a box in your room?

If you put it away carefully, you will be able to find it the next time you want it.

Put Your Doll to Bed

WHILE you are taking your nap is a good time for your doll to take her nap. Is she ready? If not, this is the time to help her get ready. Find her pajamas and gently help her undress. Then put her pajamas on and button them. Are there too many toys in her crib?

When she is ready, pull up the covers and kiss her.

Now how about you? It won't take you long, and you will be ready. Then into bed you go.

Sing a Song

DO YOU know a lot of songs you like to sing? Some are short ones. Others are long ones. Do you know a lullaby? When do you sing a lullaby?

Well—you sing a lullaby when it is time to go to sleep, and this is naptime.

Now, while you are getting undressed, sing a lullaby to yourself. By the time you finish the song I hope you are undressed and ready to climb in bed and pull the covers up. Have a good nap.

THINGS TO DO

AFTER YOUR NAP

WHEN you wake up from your nap there are many different things you can do by yourself or with your mother or a friend. Here are a few:

Make a drum and rattles

Make things with spools and pipe
cleaners

Have a doll picnic

Ride your tricycle near the house

Build cardboard block houses

Play policeman or fireman

Whether you play indoors or outdoors you can have a happy time. But when your mother calls you, what does that mean? It's time to come in, that's right. So come right in and find out what she wants. Perhaps it is something you will like.

Make a Drum

SALAD-BOWL DRUM

A piece of thin rubber or leather stretched tightly over the top of a wooden salad bowl makes a fine drum.

You and your friends will have a lot of fun walking and marching while one of you gently hits the drum with a drumstick or with your hand. If you hit too hard the drum might tear, so remember to tap it softly.

If you sit down and put the drum on your lap you can tap it with both hands.

and Rattles

RATTLES

Do you have any rattles, things that make a noise when you shake them? Do you have two rattles, or one?

This might be a good time to play with them. You can shake them as you walk. If you are outdoors you can shake them as you run. See if you can make your feet and your hands go together. Make the rattle shake with each step you take.

Rattles are fun, aren't they?

Make Things with Spools

WHEN you are alone or with others you can think of many things to make with spools and pipe cleaners.

Do you want to make a lawn mower? You will need a small spool and a pipe cleaner. Put one end of the pipe cleaner into the hole in the spool. Push it through until it comes out the other end. Now, is the spool in the middle of the pipe cleaner? Twist the two ends of the pipe cleaner together, and you have a lawn mower.

You can make the furniture and lamps you need for your dollhouse.

You can make animals, if you want to play farm or zoo.

You can make dolls of different sizes.

Try making some flowers and plants. That is fun, too.

You can play with spools and pipe cleaners on the floor, in a chair, or at a table.

If you take a long ride with your family in the car, take your spools and pipe cleaners along and think of things to make with them.

What do you always do when you are through playing with your spools and pipe cleaners? That's right, you put them away so they will be there to play with another time.

Have a Doll Picnic

IF YOU have gone on a picnic then you know that someone packs a lunch which is eaten outdoors.

Wouldn't you like to have a picnic for your dolls? You can use a box and pretend it is a picnic basket. Then make the lunch out of clay or paper. Or you can just pretend that the box is filled with good things to eat.

Where will you go for your picnic? Right over there near the wall is a good place. Do you have everything you need? How many of you will there be on this picnic? Four? Three dolls and you? No—two dolls, you and your sister. Fine. Have a good time!

Ride Your Tricycle

WHEN you and your friends ride your tricycles, where do you go?

Sometimes you ride in front of your apartment or your house.

Sometimes on the sidewalk in back.

Sometimes around the circle in the courtyard of an apartment building.

You would never go across the street or leave the block where you live, would you?

Do you want to pretend that you are the bus driver driving your bus? Be sure to stop so the people can get on the bus. When each person gets on he must pay you.

Is everyone on? Well, close the door, then, Driver, and be on your way.

Build Cardboard

CARDBOARD blocks are very sturdy, and you can have lots of fun building many different things with them. You can use shoe boxes or any other small boxes just as well. Usually the cardboard blocks are larger than solid wooden blocks, so you can make bigger buildings.

With these blocks you can build a house that is as high as you when you stand up.

Block Houses

Or, if you have a large wooden box to use as a house or barn or building, then your cardboard blocks, put end to end, make a fine fence.

Or set your blocks up so that you can use them with your dolls or stuffed animals to make a Mother Goose rhyme. Make a wall and put Humpty Dumpty on it. Put two blocks together so they make a corner and then one of your dolls can be Little Jack Horner.

You can think of many more, can't you?

Policeman or Fireman

POLICEMAN

Some policemen stand on the corner and direct traffic.

Some policemen ride motorcycles and watch the people who drive and park cars.

Some policemen drive police cars.

Which kind of policeman would you like to be? Would you like to take turns and pretend to be each one for a time?

If you are outdoors your tricycle would make a good motorcycle, wouldn't it?

What would be a good police car? How

about your wagon or tricycle or truck? You can pretend they are police cars. Be careful not to drive too fast!

FIREMAN

Have you ever made a visit to the fire department? Then you know the things that a fireman has.

Do you have a hat which you can pretend is a fireman's hat? A piece of heavy rope makes a good hose. Anything with wheels will make a fine fire engine.

Do you know all the things that a fireman does? Try some of them.

THINGS TO DO

BEFORE SUPPER

BY THIS TIME you have had a big day doing many different things. Dinner is almost ready, for soon Daddy will be coming home. Maybe your brother or sister is busy. Now what can you do alone that is fun? Try one of these:

Draw a man, using different shapes

Make a picture with your paint sticks

Build something for Daddy

Listen to a few records

Make a new puzzle

Show your dolls a book

One thing to remember is that when your mother calls you for supper it is time to stop. You can finish what you have started after supper. Maybe later you will have time to share what you have done with your daddy or mother.

Draw a Man of Shapes

ALL YOU need is one crayon and a piece of paper. It can be plain paper or newspaper.

What shape do you want the head to be? A square, a circle, or a triangle?

Now add the neck. Will it be thick or thin?

Next the body. Can you make it a different shape from the shape of the head?

You need two arms. Should they be shaped like crescents, or should they be long and thin? Now make the legs. What shape do you want them to be?

There, your man is finished. Stand back and look at him. Did you laugh? Take your picture and show it to someone, and maybe he will laugh, too.

A Paint-Stick Picture

PAINT sticks look like big fat crayons. They are different, because you dip them in water.

You can use them on paper at your easel or at a table.

How about painting a picture of your daddy or grandmother? What color paint stick will you use?

You can use paint sticks on cloth, too. Be sure to use a cloth that won't be used for anything else. You wouldn't paint on a napkin or a bed sheet or a towel. It is fun to make a design on cloth. You can make your own bedspread or a tablecloth for your dolls.

What is your design going to be?

51

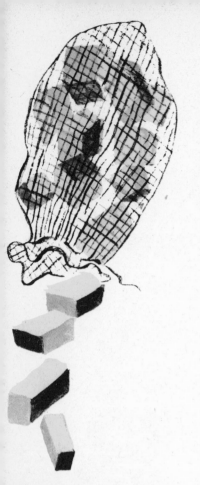

A Building for Daddy

YOU HAVE made many different things with your blocks. This time would you like to build something very special for Daddy to see when he comes home?

What do you want to build? A garage, with your cars parked inside? A stairway, with your dolls on the steps? A kitchen cupboard, table, and chairs? Beds for your dolls or cages for your animals? A fire-engine house with a sliding pole for the firemen? A street with lamp posts and traffic signs?

Stop and think. Where would be a good place, so that no one will knock over your building?

Daddy will be happy to see and hear all about the building you decide to make.

Listen to a Few Records

WHILE Mother is busy getting supper, it is a good idea for you to sit and listen to a few of your favorite records. Perhaps you are tired because you have played hard and done so many different things. If there isn't very much time left before supper you may listen to only one side of one record. If there is more time you may listen to several sides of different records.

When you listen to records, other members of the family may be doing other things. In order not to disturb them you may have to close the door to your room.

You will enjoy your records more if they don't disturb anyone else.

Which is your favorite record?

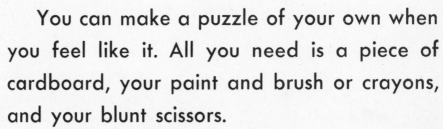

Make a New Puzzle

A **PUZZLE** is lots of fun to make. It is really a picture made of several different pieces. Each piece is a different shape and it will go in only one place in the puzzle. If you can fit all the pieces together you will have a picture. You can take the puzzle apart and put it together as often as you want.

You can make a puzzle of your own when you feel like it. All you need is a piece of cardboard, your paint and brush or crayons, and your blunt scissors.

Make a design or picture on the cardboard. Now cut the cardboard into several pieces with your blunt scissors. This may be hard work, but you will have fun doing it. How many pieces are there? Count them. Now what are you going to do? Fit them all together, and there is the picture you made!

Show Your Dolls a Book

YOU LIKE to look at books, don't you? Did you ever put all your dolls in a row and show them one of your favorite books?

First sit your dolls up. Maybe you will have to put a block behind some of them to help them sit up straight.

When all the dolls are ready, find one of your favorite books. Then sit down so that you can share the book with your dolls. Be sure to show them the pictures when you turn the pages.

They will enjoy the book.

THINGS TO DO

AFTER SUPPER

IF DADDY can play with you, maybe you can do a few things together before it is bedtime. If others are reading or watching television, you will want to play quietly, and perhaps in another room. There are lots of things you can do.

> Think of numbers
> Play with your small cars or airplanes
> Make cardboard animals
> Paste pictures in your scrapbook
> Make a picture together
> Draw or paint faces

See how many things there are to do after supper! You know many more, too. Remember you can have a very good time playing with your toys when others are busy. You try it.

Think of Numbers

YOU KNOW what numbers are, don't you? Look around and find the places where you see them.

Do you have some numbers on the front of your house? Can you say those numbers?

If you have a telephone, there are numbers on it. See if you can find and name them.

What other places would you look for numbers? A calendar? Yes, it has a number for each day of the month. And you can start with number 1 and count all the days.

A clock? It has numbers on it.

When you go to the store do you see any numbers? That's right. Almost everything they sell in the store has a number on it that tells you how much it will cost.

A thermometer has numbers to tell you how hot or cold it is.

Where do you see another number? Look at the corner of this page. Are you surprised?

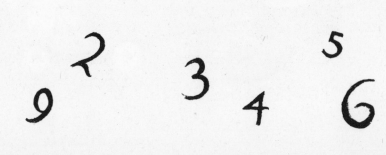

Play with Small Cars

IF YOU have a place on the rug or floor where you can play with your cars and air-planes, you can have a lot of fun playing by yourself.

You can push them along the floor just as though they were going down the street. You can make all the sounds that cars make. When you want to stop and get out of the car be sure you find a good parking place.

Now would you like to play with your air-planes? You can take one out of your pretend hangar and run it along the floor for a little way and then slowly take it up in the air. When you bring it down again be sure that it has a safe landing.

That was a good ride, wasn't it? Now where does the airplane go? Back in the hangar, of course.

Cardboard Animals

HERE is something you can do with spring clothespins and cardboard.

After supper some evening when you want to make a picture, why don't you draw it on cardboard instead of paper?

Can you draw an animal? What will it be? An elephant? A camel? A dog?

Draw just the head and the body, because you are going to use clothespins for the legs.

Now cut out what you have drawn, with your blunt scissors. Someone can help you put on a spring clothespin for the front legs and another one for the back legs.

Now your animal will stand up by itself.

Does your animal have a tail? Do you have another clothespin for that?

Paste in a Scrapbook

AFTER supper is a nice time to paste pictures in your scrapbook. Do you have a paper scrapbook or one made of cloth? Are there some empty pages in your scrapbook? If you don't have any pictures ready to paste in, why don't you make one? You can make a picture by cutting it out of paper or a magazine, or you can draw one with a crayon.

When the picture is ready, find a good place in your scrapbook. Did you find one? Now turn the picture over and put paste around the edge of the back. Next, put it on the page you have found and press it down gently. The paste will make it stick.

Another day you will want to paste more pictures in your scrapbook, so close it carefully and put it away.

Make a Picture Together

DID YOU ever make a picture with someone?

Sometimes you start the picture and someone else finishes it, and sometimes the other person starts the picture and you finish it.

Perhaps you and Mother can make one.

Do you have a paper and pencil or crayon? Do you want to start it? All right, you draw some lines. Now let Mother draw some lines. Do they look like legs, a tail, and a head? Does the picture look like a dog?

This time it is Mother's turn to start the picture. What do you think it will be? Now you finish the picture. What is it—a rabbit? A house? A boy? Now you start one more.

Draw or Paint Faces

PUTTING a face somewhere you didn't expect to find one is a great deal of fun. You can draw faces on many different things. Of course you must be careful not to put a face on something that belongs to someone else.

Do you want to use water-color paint, a crayon, or a paint stick?

Here are a few places to make a face:

On plain paper

On newspaper

On a brown paper bag

On the bottom of a paper plate

On the side or bottom of a paper cup

On a dry gourd

On a balloon

There are lots of different places. Can you think of any more?

THINGS TO DO

GOING TO BED

GOING to bed can be lots of fun if you help to make it that way. One of the best ways to help is to think of restful things to do before you get undressed. Here are some that I think you will enjoy:

Listen to a story

Listen to a music box

Listen to noises

Put one of your pictures up on the wall

Put all your things away

If you don't do any of these things, there are others to do instead. It is important to remember that you are getting ready to go to bed soon. Do something that is quiet and restful.

You have had a wonderful day because you did so many different things. Now it is time for you to sleep so that you will have a happy day tomorrow.

Listen to a Story

BEFORE going to bed is a very nice time to listen to a story. Sometimes it is fun to crawl up on Daddy's lap and listen to him read a story while he shows you the pictures.

There are other evenings when you feel like having Daddy or Mother tell you a story. When they do this, there are no pictures to see. Instead of pictures, Daddy may use his hands to show you how the story goes.

Does your sister or brother ever read a story to you?

The person who comes to take care of you when Mother and Daddy are away reads you a story before you go to bed.

When Grandmother came to visit she told a story before you went to bed? That was nice.

When the story is finished, it is time for bed. There isn't time for another story tonight. Save the next one for tomorrow night.

Listen to a Music Box

YOU LIKE music. So do I. The last thing you can do before you go to bed tonight is play your music box.

First, wind it very carefully and slowly. That is important. Then put it down gently and sit and listen. Did it play a pretty tune?

A music box plays soft music. When it first starts you can hear the music very well. Later it slows down and finally it stops.

Did you ever try to sing like a music box? You try it. Remember to sing softly.

Listen to Noises

LET'S be very quiet and just listen. Do you hear any noises?

What are some of the noises you hear when you are indoors?

A telephone bell? Yes, and it makes a loud noise.

A clock? How does the clock sound? Does it go very slowly tick-tock, or does it go very fast—tick-tick-tick? Ask someone to let you listen to a watch, and you will hear it go tick-tick-tick very fast.

Do you hear music on the radio? Sometimes it's loud music, and sometimes it is very soft music.

What are some of the noises you hear when you are outdoors?

A car or truck going by? Yes, and you know what an automobile horn sounds like, don't you? The siren on the police car or the fire truck makes a loud noise.

A train far away? Did you hear the train whistle?

An airplane high up in the sky? It makes a big noise.

A dog barking? Little dogs make a high sound and big dogs make a low sound.

Sometimes if you are very quiet you can even hear the wind.

What are some of the noises you can hear right now?

Put up a Picture

DID YOU make a picture today that you like very much? Would you like to keep it in your room? If you have a bulletin board on your wall you can tack it up there. If not, maybe you can lay it out flat on a table or the floor, and then it will be there when you wake up in the morning. Mother will help you find a place to put it.

Did someone send you a picture that you like very much? Did someone send you a post card? That would be a nice picture to have on your wall.

Put Your Things Away

LOOK around your room. Are there any of your things on the floor? Pick each one up and put it where it belongs, on your shelf or in your toy box. Things can't be left on the floor at night. Everything must be put away.

Now, are you finished and ready to undress? Are your pajamas and bedroom slippers near by?

Did you hang up your clothes and brush your teeth?

Where are you now?

THINGS TO DO

CS 7-54   Printed in U.S.A.   20-50

Date Due